THIS LAND CALLED AMERICA: **OKLAHOMA**

CREATIVE EDUCATION

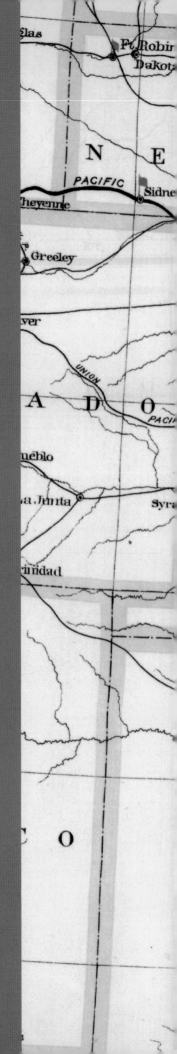

Published by Creative Education
P.O. Box 227, Mankato, Minnesota 56002
Creative Education is an imprint of The Creative Company
www.thecreativecompany.us

Design by Blue Design (www.bluedes.com)
Art direction by Rita Marshall
Book production by The Design Lab
Printed in the United States of America

Photographs by Alamy (John Elk III, Betty LaRue, Papilio, Chuck Place,
Tom Till), Corbis (William A. Bake, Bettmann, Lindsay Hebberd, Arthur
Morris, David Muench, Louie Psihoyos, Arthur Rothstein, Richard Hamilton
Smith), Getty Images (Jed Jacobsohn, NOAA Photo Library, Eric O'Connell,
Popperfoto, Brandi Simons)

Library of Congress Cataloging-in-Publication Data
Gish, Melissa.
Oklahoma / by Melissa Gish.
p. cm. — (This land called America)
Includes bibliographical references and index.
ISBN 978-1-58341-789-8
1. Oklahoma—Juvenile literature. I. Title. II. Series.
F694.3.G57 2009
976.6—dc22          2008009519

First Edition
9 8 7 6 5 4 3 2 1

*This Land Called America*
# OKLAHOMA
Melissa Gish

# Oklahoma

MELISSA GISH

A SEPTEMBER BREEZE RUSTLES THROUGH
GOLDEN WHEAT FIELDS NEAR AN OUTDOOR
ARENA IN OKLAHOMA. THE SHARP SMELLS OF
CATTLE AND HORSES FILL THE AIR. CRASHES
ECHO THROUGH THE STANDS. IN A NARROW
PEN, A RESTLESS BULL JERKS ANGRILY. THE
CROWD WATCHES A YOUNG COWBOY SLIDE
INTO THE PEN AND SIT ON THE BULL'S BACK.
A ROPE HAS BEEN TIED TO THE BULL. THE
COWBOY WRAPS THE ROPE AROUND HIS HAND,
PULLING IT TIGHT. HE GIVES A QUICK NOD, THE
PEN DOOR OPENS, AND THE CROWD BURSTS
INTO CHEERS. THE BULL KICKS AND SPINS,
BUT THE COWBOY HOLDS ON TIGHT. THIS IS
OKLAHOMA RODEO AT ITS BEST.

YEAR
1541
Spanish adventurer Francisco Vásquez de Coronado first explores the land now called Oklahoma.
EVENT

# Bountiful Prairie

Centuries ago, the land that is now Oklahoma was a wilderness of mountains, valleys, and grassy plains. The earliest explorers were Spaniards seeking gold. They traveled north from Mexico in the 1500s but did not stay in Oklahoma. In 1541, Francisco Vásquez de Coronado claimed the land for Spain.

About 100 years later, French explorers traveled south from Canada. In 1682, René-Robert de La Salle claimed Oklahoma for France. He and other explorers found bands of American Indians, including the Wichita, Osage, and Pawnee, who raised crops, trapped beavers, and hunted buffalo. The Indians traded furs with the French.

As the French expanded their fur trade in the area, the Spanish returned. For many years, France and Spain fought for control over the land. In 1800, the Spanish gave up and left Oklahoma.

Then, in 1803, Napoleon Bonaparte of France sold Oklahoma to United States president Thomas Jefferson as part of the Louisiana Territory. Jefferson sent many men on trips to learn about the land and its native inhabitants. These men drew maps and set up travel routes through the Louisiana Territory.

*When Francisco Coronado's expedition (opposite) arrived in Oklahoma, they found many Indians of the Pawnee tribe (above).*

YEAR
1682     French explorer and fur trader René-Robert de La Salle claims Oklahoma for France.
EVENT

- 7 -

Slavery was common
in the frontier lands of
Indian Territory; but
after the American Civil
War, freed slaves created
many all-black towns in
Oklahoma.

State bird: scissor-tailed flycatcher

Settlers moved westward. By the early 1800s, American Indians all across the U.S. were being forced from their homes to make room for the white settlers. The U.S. government thought Oklahoma would be a good place to relocate the Indians. They called the land Indian Territory. To get to Indian Territory, many Indians followed a route called the Trail of Tears. Thousands of people died along the way.

Those American Indians who survived settled the new area and began raising cattle and pigs and growing crops. They set up many towns in Indian Territory that still exist today. For example, Tulsa was first settled by the Creek people. Ardmore was established by the Chickasaw, and Tahlequah was founded by the Cherokee.

The first railroad to completely cross Oklahoma was finished in 1872. Cowboys and cattlemen followed soon after. They brought their animals to Oklahoma to graze on the grasslands. Fattened herds were driven to market through Oklahoma on the famous Chisholm Trail, which ran from the Red River in southern Texas to Abilene, Kansas.

The U.S. government at first told the Indians that it would not sell the land in Indian Territory to settlers. But in 1889, the government took almost two million acres (809,370 ha) from the Creek and Seminole peoples. So many settlers wanted

YEAR
1803    France sells the Louisiana Territory, including Oklahoma, to the U.S.
EVENT

a part of that land that people raced each other to claim property in contests called land runs or land rushes.

The first Oklahoma land run was held on April 22, 1889. More than 50,000 settlers lined up at the starting line, each wanting to stake a claim. People who cheated and started racing ahead of time were nicknamed "Sooners." After Oklahoma became the 46th state on November 16, 1907, it adopted the nickname "The Sooner State."

During World War I, which was fought from 1914 to 1918, Oklahoma produced a lot of food and oil for the American military. But when the war was over, crop and oil prices fell, and many Oklahomans became very poor. They suffered through the Great Depression in the 1930s. Fortunately, after the Depression ended, Oklahoma once again became a leader in oil production.

*Oklahoma women raised their families and helped get schools and churches built near the oil fields in the 1940s..*

YEAR

1872    The Missouri-Kansas-Texas Railroad (called Katy) becomes the first to cross Oklahoma.

EVENT

- 10 -

# Prairies and Mountains

OKLAHOMA IS PART OF A REGION IN THE MIDDLE OF
AMERICA CALLED THE GREAT PLAINS. MOST OF THE
STATE'S NORTHERN BORDER TOUCHES KANSAS. ITS
NEIGHBORS TO THE EAST ARE ARKANSAS AND MISSOURI.
IT IS BORDERED ON THE SOUTH BY TEXAS. OKLAHOMA'S
PANHANDLE—A LONG, NARROW PIECE OF LAND THAT JUTS

farther to the west than the rest of the state—touches New Mexico and Colorado. The Oklahoma landscape is marked by rivers, valleys, mountains, and plains.

Rivers flow through steep valleys and around broad, flat highlands in the Ozark Plateau, a region in northeastern Oklahoma. To the south and west of the Ozark Plateau, the land flattens out in a large prairie. Farmers grow corn and soybeans, and ranchers raise cattle on these plains. Oil and coal are produced there as well.

A number of mountain ranges, including the Ouachita (*wah-SHEE-tah*) Mountains, can be found in southern Oklahoma. Streams flow through the valleys between these rough sandstone ridges. Once, these mountains were probably as tall as the Rocky Mountains—more than 14,000 feet (4,270 m) high. Now, after millions of years, the highest mountain in the Ouachitas is only 2,950 feet (899 m) tall. They are the only major mountains on the Great Plains.

*Oklahoma is known for its rolling prairies (opposite) and the Ouachita Mountains (above), home to more than a dozen plants found nowhere else on Earth.*

YEAR

1897  The Nellie Johnstone oil well in Bartlesville becomes the first flowing commercial oil well in the world.

EVENT

The Arbuckle Mountains are a small range in south-central Oklahoma. Cattle often graze on the slopes of these low, grassy mountains. The Wichita Mountains are located in the southwestern part of the state. They include a 59,020-acre (23,885 ha) wildlife refuge that is home to elk and buffalo.

Scattered forests cover the rolling prairie of the Red River Valley along the Texas border. Farmers grow vegetables, peanuts, and cotton there. North of the Red River toward the Kansas border, the land completely changes. In the region known as the Sandstone Hills, rocky mounds rise 250 to 400 feet (76–122 m) into the air. The land is dotted with small forests of short trees that grow well in poor soil.

---

*White-tailed deer (above) are some of the animals given safe haven in the Wichita Mountains Wildlife Refuge (opposite), which is also home to a rare mixed-grass prairie protected by the rocks.*

1907     Oklahoma becomes the 46th state on November 16.

*Over millions of years,
wind and water shaped
the volcanic rock at
Black Mesa State Park
into unique formations.*

The Red Beds Plains cover the state west of the Sandstone Hills straight down to the Texas border. A small portion on the east side of the Plains is forested, but most of this region is covered in grassland. To the west are the Gypsum Hills, which stand 150 to 200 feet (45–60 m) high. Gypsum is a white mineral that looks like glass. The Gypsum Hills are also called the Glass Hills.

Oklahoma's panhandle is a dry, nearly treeless area of land. Called the High Plains, this region includes Black Mesa. At 4,973 feet (1,516 m) tall, this rock formation is the highest point in Oklahoma.

There's no mistaking the change of seasons in Oklahoma. Winters are cold, with temperatures dropping to around 20 to 30 °F (-1 to -7 °C). Summers are hot, with average temperatures around 80 °F (27 °C). Summers are also the time of year when tornadoes are at their worst in Oklahoma.

Much of Oklahoma is located in the center of what is known as Tornado Alley. This is the area of America where the strongest tornadoes occur most often. Oklahoma has suffered thousands of tornadoes. One of the worst tornadoes in the state's history occurred on April 9, 1947. The storm killed 101 people and injured 782 others.

*With 54 "twisters," Oklahoma is second only to Texas in the average number of tornadoes predicted to occur each year.*

YEAR

1909    The first Boy Scout troop in America is established in Pawhuska.

EVENT

# Native Pride

TODAY, MORE THAN THREE-QUARTERS OF OKLAHOMA'S PEOPLE ARE WHITE. AMERICAN INDIANS AND AFRICAN AMERICANS EACH MAKE UP ABOUT EIGHT PERCENT OF THE POPULATION. PEOPLE OF HISPANIC OR LATINO ORIGIN ACCOUNT FOR ALMOST SEVEN PERCENT. ASIAN AMERICANS ARE THE SMALLEST ETHNIC GROUP.

Oklahoma's first African Americans came to Indian Territory with relocated American Indians. Many had been slaves in America's southern states. Later, they arrived as settlers and cowboys. During the American Civil War between the North and the South, African American soldiers served with the Northern, anti-slavery states. After the war ended in 1865, some of these soldiers built forts and worked to enforce the laws of Indian Territory. The American Indians nicknamed them "Buffalo Soldiers."

Sixty-seven American Indian tribes originally lived in Indian Territory. Today, many of those people's descendants still live in Oklahoma. In fact, Oklahoma contains the second-largest population of American Indians in the U.S. In Oklahoma, Indians have played a significant role in everything from politics to entertainment to sports.

*The Creek Council House, the capitol of the Creek Nation, was rebuilt in stone in 1878 and is now a museum.*

*The average farm in Oklahoma is about 400 acres (161 ha), and the top crops are corn, cotton, and wheat (opposite).*

YEAR

1917   The Phillips Petroleum Company (now ConocoPhillips) is founded by brothers L. E. and Frank Phillips.

EVENT

*Pretty Boy Floyd earned his nickname after his first robbery, when he was described to police as a "pretty boy."*

A Cherokee named Wilma Mankiller was born in Tahlequah, Oklahoma, in 1945. In 1987, Mankiller was elected the first female chief of the Cherokee Nation. She opened the door of opportunity for other Indian women to become leaders.

Will Rogers is known as Oklahoma's favorite son. A Cherokee American who was born in Indian Territory, Rogers grew up wanting to be a cowboy. He first entertained people with horse and rope tricks. Later, he became a movie and radio star. By the 1930s, nearly everyone in America knew his name.

Oklahoman Jim Thorpe was also part Indian. Thorpe was one of the most famous athletes of all time. His 20-year athletic career began in 1907. He won Olympic gold medals in track and field, and he played professional football, baseball, and basketball.

Not all Oklahomans are famous for being good, though—some are known for being bad. Charles "Pretty Boy" Floyd was a bank robber who was hated by the police but loved by locals in his Oklahoma home region. During the 1920s and '30s, many people did not trust banks and were glad that Floyd robbed them. Some called him "the Robin Hood of the Cookson Hills."

*Athlete Jim Thorpe grew up with the Sac and Fox name of Wa-Tho-Huk, meaning "Bright Path."*

YEAR
1925   The Oklahoma Forest Commission is created to protect the state's forest resources.
EVENT

- *20* -

The first people who worked in Oklahoma were farmers and ranchers. Since the state's early days, agriculture has continued to expand. Today, Oklahoma ranks high among all states in cattle and wheat production. Other products include poultry, pigs, and dairy. Almost 90,000 farms cover the state.

When oil and natural gas were discovered in Oklahoma in the late 1800s, people flocked to the area to seek their fortunes. Drilling in the earth for natural resources such as oil continues today, and many energy companies are located in Oklahoma. Today, Oklahoma's state government sponsors programs to study ethanol, a fuel made from plants instead of oil.

*Oil production (opposite) and beef cattle (above) are two big moneymakers.*

YEAR

1926    Miss Tulsa, Norma Smallwood, is the first American Indian to be crowned Miss America.

EVENT

Thne aerospace industry is now bigger than the energy industry in Oklahoma. Hundreds of companies maintain and upgrade airplanes and build airplane parts. Oklahoma manufacturers make tires and air conditioners, while other companies research the weather.

When they are not working, Oklahomans like to celebrate their cultural heritage. American Indian powwows invite people to sing, dance, and celebrate the native culture. Rodeos showcase cowboys who rope calves, wrestle steers, and ride bulls and bucking broncos.

*Technology and tradition mix in Oklahoma, with workers at airplane parts facilities operating machinery (above), while dancers gather at such events as an Anadarko Kiowa ceremony (opposite).*

The first parking meter is invented by Carl C. Magee and installed in Oklahoma City.

# Western Heritage

Oklahomans have experienced hardship in their history. The state suffered during a period of severe drought and windstorms in the 1930s. Many people lost their farms in areas of Oklahoma's plains that came to be known as the Dust Bowl.

The Field of Empty
Chairs memorial
represents the people
who died in the 1995
Oklahoma City
bombing.

Despite such difficult times, agriculture survived, and today, wheat fields and cattle ranches mark Oklahoma's landscape. So do pumpjacks. These machines bob up and down, drawing oil from deep in the earth. Oil wells are drilled virtually everywhere. In fact, Oklahoma City has the only state capitol with an oil rig on its grounds.

Oklahoma City also boasts the Gold Dome, a spectacular dome-shaped building with 625 gold-coated aluminum panels that span 145 feet (44 m) across its roof. First designed as a bank, the building now houses many businesses and organizations. Nearby, the National Cowboy & Western Heritage Museum displays more than 28,000 artifacts and works of art.

*Many families were forced to abandon their sand-buried homes in Oklahoma's Dust Bowl area.*

A more solemn Oklahoma City monument stands at the site of the former Alfred P. Murrah Federal Building, which was bombed in 1995. The national memorial, built on the site of the destroyed building, honors the 168 people who were killed, along with the survivors and rescuers.

*Route 66 had several nicknames and was sometimes called "The Mother Road" or "Will Rogers Highway."*

On both sides of Oklahoma City, drivers can cruise the historic Route 66 highway. The U.S. government established this highway in 1926 to expand tourism throughout the West. In the 1960s, interstate freeways replaced most of Route 66. The road still exists, but it no longer appears on most maps.

Oklahoma's natural resources also draw visitors to the state. The state ranks first in the U.S. in its number of man-made lakes. Covering more than 102,000 acres (41,278 ha), Lake Eufaula is the largest in the state.

Oklahomans love college sports. Whether it's baseball, football, or basketball, tens of thousands of fans gather in the city of Norman to watch the University of Oklahoma Sooners. The Oklahoma State University Cowboys and Cowgirls entertain fans in Stillwater.

Oklahoma has two minor-league baseball teams as well: the Tulsa Drillers and the Oklahoma RedHawks. Oklahoma City is home to the Central Hockey League's Blazers and a National Women's Football Association team, the Lightning.

For a time, Oklahoma opened its doors to the National Basketball Association's (NBA) New Orleans Hornets when New Orleans was devastated by Hurricane Katrina in 2005.

*Sooners athletes have a reputation for being winners; the school has earned 25 national championships.*

YEAR

1993   The Oklahoma Quality Jobs Program is established to encourage people to find jobs in the state.

EVENT

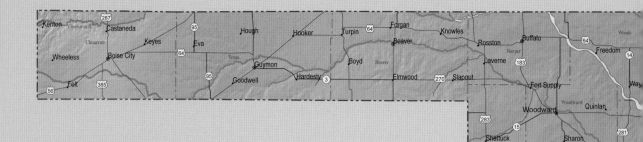

## QUICK FACTS

Population: 3,617,316

Largest city: Oklahoma City (pop. 547,274)

Capital: Oklahoma City

Entered the union: November 16, 1907

Nickname: Sooner State

State flower: mistletoe

State bird: scissor-tailed flycatcher

Size: 69,898 sq mi (181,035 sq km)—20th-biggest in U.S.

Major industries: farming, cattle, oil, natural gas

From 2005 to 2007, the New Orleans/Oklahoma City Hornets played 71 home games in Oklahoma City before moving back to Louisiana. In 2008, the NBA announced that the Seattle SuperSonics franchise would relocate to Oklahoma City and be renamed the Thunder, thus giving the state a permanent stake in professional basketball.

A more traditional Oklahoma sport is the rodeo. The largest rodeo in America is held every year during Pioneer Days in Guymon. More than 900 people compete in the rodeo. Farther east, travelers to Quapaw can see the oldest powwow in the nation. Held each July 4, this ceremony has been celebrated for more than 135 years.

Oklahomans are proud of their state's Western heritage. This can be seen in local artist Paul Moore's bronze sculptures

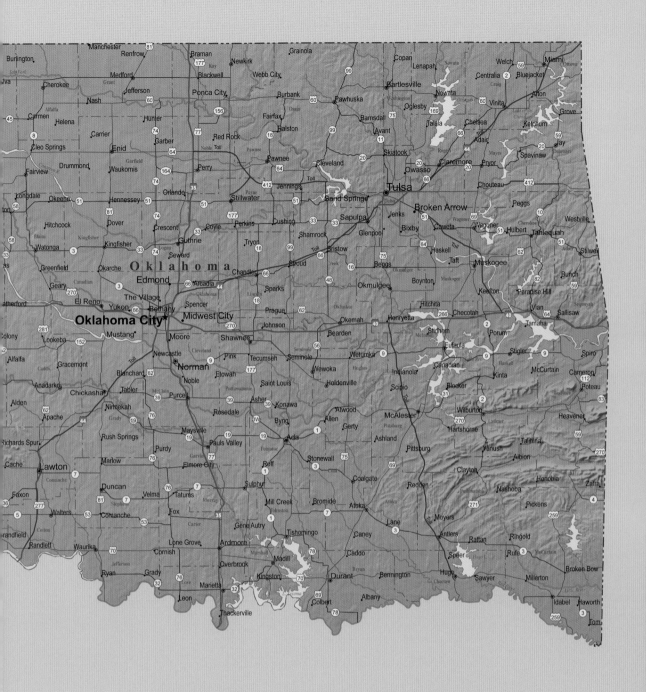

celebrating the Land Run of 1889. Commissioned in 2007, the
365-foot-long (111 m) monument will depict horses and riders
ready to race for Oklahoma's land. Standing in Oklahoma
City, the monumental work is just one way that Oklahomans
will keep their state's history alive as they continue to move
into the future.

# BIBLIOGRAPHY

Gibson, Arrell Morgan. *Oklahoma: A History of Five Centuries.* Norman, Okla.: University of Oklahoma Press, 1981.

Joyce, Davis D., ed. *"An Oklahoma I Had Never Seen Before": Alternative Views of Oklahoma History.* Norman, Okla.: University of Oklahoma Press, 1998.

Lynn-Sherow, Bonnie. *Red Earth: Race and Agriculture in Oklahoma Territory.* Lawrence, Kans.: University Press of Kansas, 2004.

Oklahoma Department of Tourism and Recreation. "A Look at Oklahoma: Oklahoma's History." Oklahoma State History and Information. http://www.ok.gov/osfdocs/stinfo2.html.

Witzel, Michael Karl, and Gyvel Young-Witzel. *Legendary Route 66: A Journey through Time along America's Mother Road.* Minneapolis: Voyageur Press, 2007.

# INDEX